Why Do I Feel So Sad?

Why Do I Feel So Sad?

A GRIEF BOOK FOR CHILDREN

WRITTEN BY Tracy Lambert, LPC
ILLUSTRATED BY Elena Napoli

ROCKRIDGE
PRESS

For general information on our other products and services or to obtain technical support, please contact our Customer Care Department within the United States at (866) 744-2665, or outside the United States at (510) 253-0500.

Rockridge Press publishes its books in a variety of electronic and print formats. Some content that appears in print may not be available in electronic books, and vice versa.

TRADEMARKS: Rockridge Press and the Rockridge Press logo are trademarks or registered trademarks of Callisto Media Inc. and/or its affiliates, in the United States and other countries, and may not be used without written permission. All other trademarks are the property of their respective owners. Rockridge Press is not associated with any product or vendor mentioned in this book.

Interior and Cover Designer: Heather Krakora
Art Producer: Sue Bischofberger
Editor: Seth Schwartz
Production Manager: Riley Hoffman
Production Editor: Chris Gage
Illustrations © Elena Napoli, 2020
Author photo courtesy of Stephanie Clark

ISBN: Print 978-1-64611-713-0 | eBook 978-1-64611-714-7

R0

To my loving husband, Josh, you're my favorite.
Mom and Granny, thank you for everything,
I am who I am because of you.
To Papa, always in my heart.

– TL

To those friends
who support you, no matter what.
To those friends
who make you laugh every time you're sad.
To all my friends,
without whom the days would be
way less colorful.

– EN

There are times when
your life may be hard.

Grief is a strong and powerful feeling
that comes after a loss or big change in life.

When grief happens, it makes our lives feel different than before.

People feel grief for many different reasons.

My Grandpa has died.

My dog ran away from home and didn't come back.

My parents aren't married anymore.

I had to move away
to a new home and school this year.

I don't have as many friends as I used to.

HOW ABOUT YOU?

Have you or someone you know
ever felt grief before?

Adults feel grief, too.
You may see
adults crying more
or not smiling as much.
They may have a hard time
doing their job or
seem sad a lot
of the time.

Every person feels grief differently in their body and mind.

You may feel sad a lot or cry more than usual.

You may not want to do
your favorite things,
like playing, dancing, or
watching TV.

You might feel worried that this loss will happen again or feel lonely a lot of the time.

You may feel like
you don't want to think
or talk about this loss at all.

You may notice your head hurting or
your heart beating really fast.

You may have a tight or upset stomach.

You may feel mad a lot of the time
and not know why.

You might have trouble listening or paying attention at school.

You might feel scared
you did something
to cause the loss.

You may find it hard
to fall or stay asleep.

You may feel quiet
and not talk as much.

SCARED GUILT

You may feel some
or many of these feelings
at different times—
at school, at home, or
out in public.

SAD

WORRY

Just remember, it is normal
to have these feelings during grief.

HOW ABOUT YOU?
What feelings or changes have you had during grief?

Grief can feel huge or small in your life.

It is normal to feel better sometimes
and then have some of these feelings come back.

You may wonder
when life will feel happy again.
Here are some things
you can do to feel better
about your grief.

Talk to an adult you trust,
like a parent, teacher,
or counselor.

Express how you are feeling by drawing,

playing, or through music.

Move your body!

Try walking, playing sports, riding a bike, or dancing.

Find ways to say goodbye, like attending or creating a memorial, writing a letter, or making a book of memories.

Let your friends know
how you are feeling.
Everyone feels grief
at some time in their life.

It helps to understand and talk about it.

HOW ABOUT YOU?

What would you do
when feeling grief?

Everyone needs support and to know that they are not alone!

GRIEF RESOURCES FOR KIDS

Activities

Here are some activities you can do by yourself or with an adult to feel better about your grief.

CREATE A MEMORY BOOK

1. Ask an adult to help find a scrapbook to put photos into.

2. Think about memories that feel important and that you want to keep forever. You could find pictures of your loved one or of your favorite things you did together.

3. Write words about each memory or how the memory makes you feel.

4. Don't forget you can decorate the outside of your book with words, pictures, or stickers, too!

DRAW YOUR FEELINGS

Have an adult draw or print out an outlined body shape for you. Think about where you are feeling your grief the most and color or draw in those parts of the body. You can also write words about your feelings, too.

FINISH THE FEELING SENTENCE

It is helpful to think about our feelings in different ways. Try writing or sharing your answers with someone you trust for these sentences:

"What I feel most sad about right now is … "

"What I worry about sometimes is … "

"Something that helps me feel better is … "

"Two ways I can share my feelings are … "

MY HEART STORY

1. Using a sheet of construction paper, cut out a shape of a big heart (or have an adult help you).

2. On one side of the heart, draw yourself or your family before the loss. You can also write words about your feelings, too!

3. Flip the heart over, and draw how you or your life looks different.

4. Try talking about or telling a story about both sides of your heart and how it may be feeling different now.

Websites & Apps

Sesame Street in Communities is a fantastic website for parents and children dealing with many life challenges. There is a specific page for grief support and Sesame Street videos discussing the topics of death, loss, and grief.

> SesameStreetinCommunities.org/topics/grief

PBS Kids has a family health page, focusing on resilience. This includes information on supporting children through various loss and trauma experiences, including natural disasters and public loss tragedies.

> PBSKids.org/arthur/health/resilience

Calm App focuses on mindfulness, meditation, and relaxation. There are some soothing stories for kids that can assist in calming for bedtime or when they may be feeling overwhelmed with emotion. This is available for download on a phone or tablet.

DreamyKid Meditation App is easy to use and offers many calming mindfulness exercises. The app provides meditation activities, guided imagery techniques, and affirmations.

GRIEF RESOURCES FOR PARENTS

Talking to Children About Grief

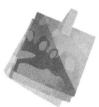

It can be difficult to know the right words to use when talking with your child about death, loss, and the grief they may be feeling. Actively listening to your child during this time is important, since they may feel confused or be curious about the loss.

Here are some things to try when talking to your child about loss and grief:

⇒ Answer questions directly and avoid using phrases that may be confusing, such as "They passed away," or "They're in a better place now."

⇒ When giving direct statements about death, you can try using:
  ✳ "Death happens to all animals and humans when our bodies and minds stop working."
  ✳ "When someone dies, they don't need to eat or sleep and they don't come back."

⇒ Validate their emotions and remind them feeling this way is completely normal.

⇒ Remind the child they are safe and will always be cared for! Many children dealing with loss can feel disconnected while family members are dealing with their own grief as well. Verbalizing this support will help them feel stable and secure.

⇒ Don't stifle your own emotions during this time, since you may be grieving as well! It is healthy to model emotional expression to children.

⇒ Many children feel worried about discussing the loss because of making someone else feel sad. It is helpful to encourage talking about the grief experience and using statements of emotion. Try using statements such as:
  ✳ "I feel sad when I think about how much I miss them, but I am happy we can talk about this together."
  ✳ "It's okay to cry when we talk about these things together; it is normal if that happens."

⇒ Lastly, don't forget support for yourself! When facing a loss in life, it is easy to get caught up in caring for everyone around us and not ourselves. Utilize the resources to find a grief support group or a therapist to speak with.

Organizations

Here are a few resources for additional information on talking with and supporting your child that is grieving:

National Alliance for Grieving Children is a great organization providing information on childhood grief, support activities, and ways to connect to local resources.
ChildrenGrieve.org

Child Mind Institute has a vast library of resources, guides, and articles in supporting children and families through many life challenges.
ChildMind.org/article/helping-children-deal-grief

The Dougy Center: The National Center for Grieving Children & Families has articles, books, and videos focusing on children experiencing grief. Their school and community toolkit is helpful for coping skills, podcasts on grief, and support activities.
TDCSchoolToolKit.org/kids

Books

When Children Grieve: For Adults to Help Children Deal with Death, Divorce, Pet Loss, Moving, and Other Losses, by John W. James
This book provides an overview of ways to support your child through various grief experiences.

It's OK That You're Not OK: Meeting Grief and Loss in a Culture That Doesn't Understand, by Megan Devine
This is a fantastic book for normalizing and validating emotions within the grief process. It can serve as a support to learn more about your own grief and help you better understand the experience your child may be going through.

ABOUT THE AUTHOR

Tracy Lambert is a licensed professional counselor in private practice located in a suburb of Houston, Texas. She obtained her master's degree in clinical psychology with a counseling specialization from The Chicago School of Professional Psychology. Tracy specializes in working with children, adolescents, and their families dealing with anxiety, grief, and loss.

ABOUT THE ILLUSTRATOR

Elena Napoli is an Italian illustrator and character designer who studied entertainment design at the NEMO Academy of Digital Arts in Florence. Growing up in the Italian art scene, she has drawn for as long as she can remember, and her greatest passion has always been children's illustration. Elena dreams of travelling, doing what she loves, and finding her place in the world.

Printed in the USA
CPSIA information can be obtained
at www.ICGtesting.com
CBHW040753010624
9306CB00022B/110

9 781646 117130